While walking home from softball practice with her dog Dignity,
Noah is startled by a woman laying on the sidewalk.

The woman's pants are too short and worn. She can see socks through the holes in the woman's shoes. She is lying on the ground with her head on a suitcase.

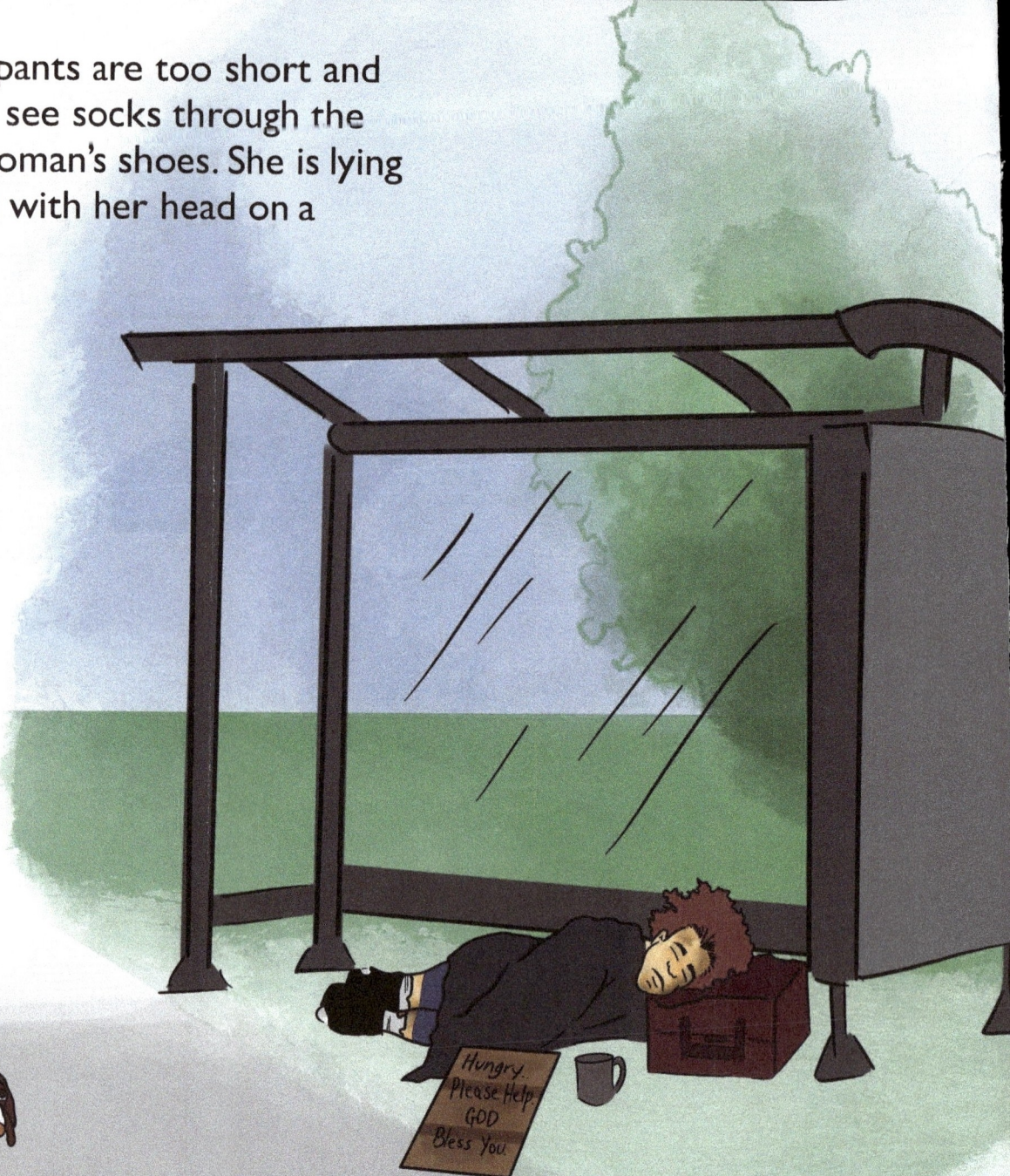

Propped up against her is a piece of cardboard with a cup in front which reads, "Hungry. Please help. God bless you."

Noah read the sign, thought about what it meant for a bit, and then kept walking home.

The woman's eyes were closed so she didn't see Noah, but she probably heard her and Dignity walking by.

When Noah got home, she immediately looked for her Mom to talk about what she saw.

"Mom! Mom! Where are you?" She yelled.

"I'm here!" Ms. Worthy yelled back. "I'm in the kitchen!"

"Mom, when we were walking home, Dignity and I saw a woman sleeping on the ground." Her clothes were all mismatched and she didn't smell too good."

"Oh?" Ms. Worthy responded.

Noah continued, "Why was she sleeping on the ground? Doesn't she have somewhere else she could sleep? Somewhere else she could go?"

"Noah, it sounds like you may have just seen someone who doesn't have a place to live. Someone who may not have a home. A person who is experiencing homelessness. Do you know what that means?"

"You mean she doesn't have a home she can go to like me?"

"Right."

"Why not?" Noah asked.

"Well, there are lots of reasons why someone might be sleeping outside or experiencing homelessness. Sometimes the home where they used to live is not safe. Sometimes they don't have the money to pay for a place to live. Or they are working, yet still don't have enough money. Sometimes they are sick and have a hard time keeping a job."

She continued, **"You don't know someone's story until you talk to them**. Now, if they are willing to tell you, that's great, but sometimes they may not want to. That's okay too. You know, it's not always important that we know everyone's business, but it is important to know what we can do to help."

She asked Noah, "So what do you think we can do to help? Do you want to help?"

Noah replied enthusiastically, "Yes!
Yes, I want to help Mom! I'm sad that
she's sleeping on the streets."

Ms. Worthy said, **"Oftentimes, the person needing help
can communicate exactly what they need. We don't
need to guess. Sometimes we ask and they tell us.
Sometimes they put it on a sign."**

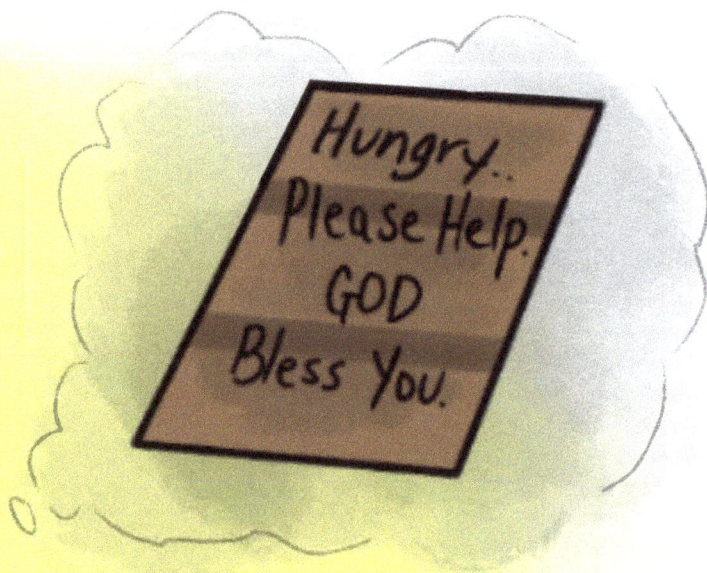

Hungry..
Please Help.
GOD
Bless You.

Noah perked up, "Yes! She had a sign!
It said "Hungry. Please help.
God bless you.""

"Ah well, she's telling us what she needs. We should listen to her. **And we can also listen with our eyes.**"

"What does that mean Mom? How do we listen with our eyes?"

"Well, let's play a little game. What do you think is going on if you see me do this?"

"Oh! Oh, I know! You're cold! I can see that you are cold."

Noah looks at Dignity, "Well I could give her some gloves, or a hat, or a coat, and some hot cocoa."

"Yes, let's go do that right now. Let's look in our closet and see what hats, coats, and gloves we can give."

Noah ran to the hall closet to pull out items they could give to someone in need.

After finding several items, she went back to her mom and said, "What else?"

Ms. Worthy said, **"Well, we can go through our clothes to help others too, but let's get back to the sign you saw. What did it say again?**

It said, "Hungry. Please help. God bless you."

"Do you think we should get her something to eat?"

"Yes!"

"You say she was sleeping on the ground. If you listen with your eyes, what would you say she might need? Is sleeping on the ground comfortable?"

"No, it's not. Whenever I even lay on the floor in here I at least need a blanket or a pillow...

Ohhhh..."

A lightbulb went off in Noah's head!

She continued, "Maybe she would like a pillow or a blanket or something soft?"

"Maybe. We won't know unless we ask her. Would you like to ask her?"

"Well, I'm scared to ask her alone." Noah said with her head down.

"Noah, at your age I wouldn't want you talking to strangers. It's totally okay to be a little afraid of talking to an adult that you do not know. Let's go together. What do you think?"

Noah nodded, "Yes."

They got some pre-packaged snacks and fruit from the kitchen. Noah grabbed an extra blanket from the living room. Then Noah, Dignity, and Ms. Worthy all set out to talk to the woman that was sleeping on the street.

When they got back to the location where the woman was sleeping, Noah found her awake and sitting upright. She had a smile on her face.

Ms. Worthy smiled back and spoke first, holding out the fruit and snacks.

"Hello," Ms. Worthy said.

"Hello," the woman replied.

"Would you like some snacks?"

"Oh yes, thank you, God bless you."

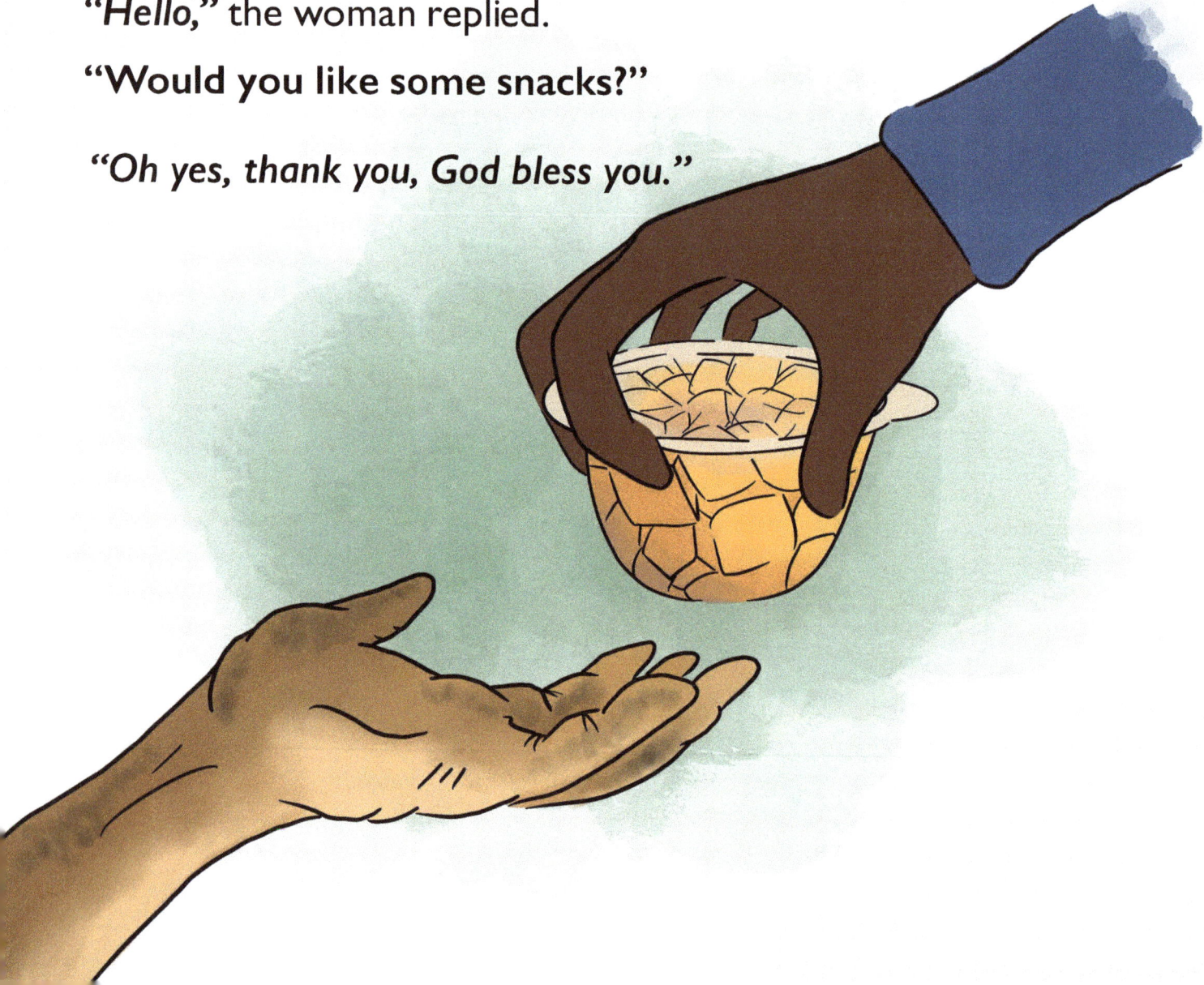

"I'm Monique Worthy. This is my daughter Noah, and our dog Dignity. My daughter saw you earlier today and you have been on her mind ever since."

"Oh! Oh, my dear, what's on your mind?"

Noah responded, "Well your sign said you were hungry, so we brought you some food. Plus, I don't think sleeping on the street is comfortable, so we brought you this blanket. Is there anything else that you need?"

"Wow. Oh wow. Sweet girl, no one ever stops and takes the time to ask me what I need. **Most people just throw their loose change my way and act like they don't even see me.** I thank you for the food and the blanket. I could really use some water and fresh socks."

"We can help with that. Right mom?", Noah asked.

"Absolutely. We'll bring it to you. Also, would you like a hot meal?" Ms. Worthy points to a local restaurant.

"Oh that would be wonderful. I'll save the snacks and fruit for later." The woman replied.

"One more thing? What is your name?"

Tears glistened in the woman's eyes.

"Oh no. What's wrong? We didn't mean to upset you." Noah said.

"My goodness, you didn't do anything wrong. I'm just so touched that you asked me my name. **No one ever asks my name. All I want sometimes is simply to be treated like everyone else, to be treated like a whole person**. I wasn't always living on the street, you know?

Anyway, I'm Nicole."

"Nicole. I like that name." Noah said sweetly.

"It's nice to meet you, Nicole," said Ms. Worthy.

"Nice to meet you as well. This is the most conversation I've had all week. Thank you."

"It's our pleasure."

With that, Ms. Worthy, Noah, and Dignity were on their way. They purchased some hot food for Nicole along with a gift card so she could get some more hot food later. They also brought back some new socks and bottled water.

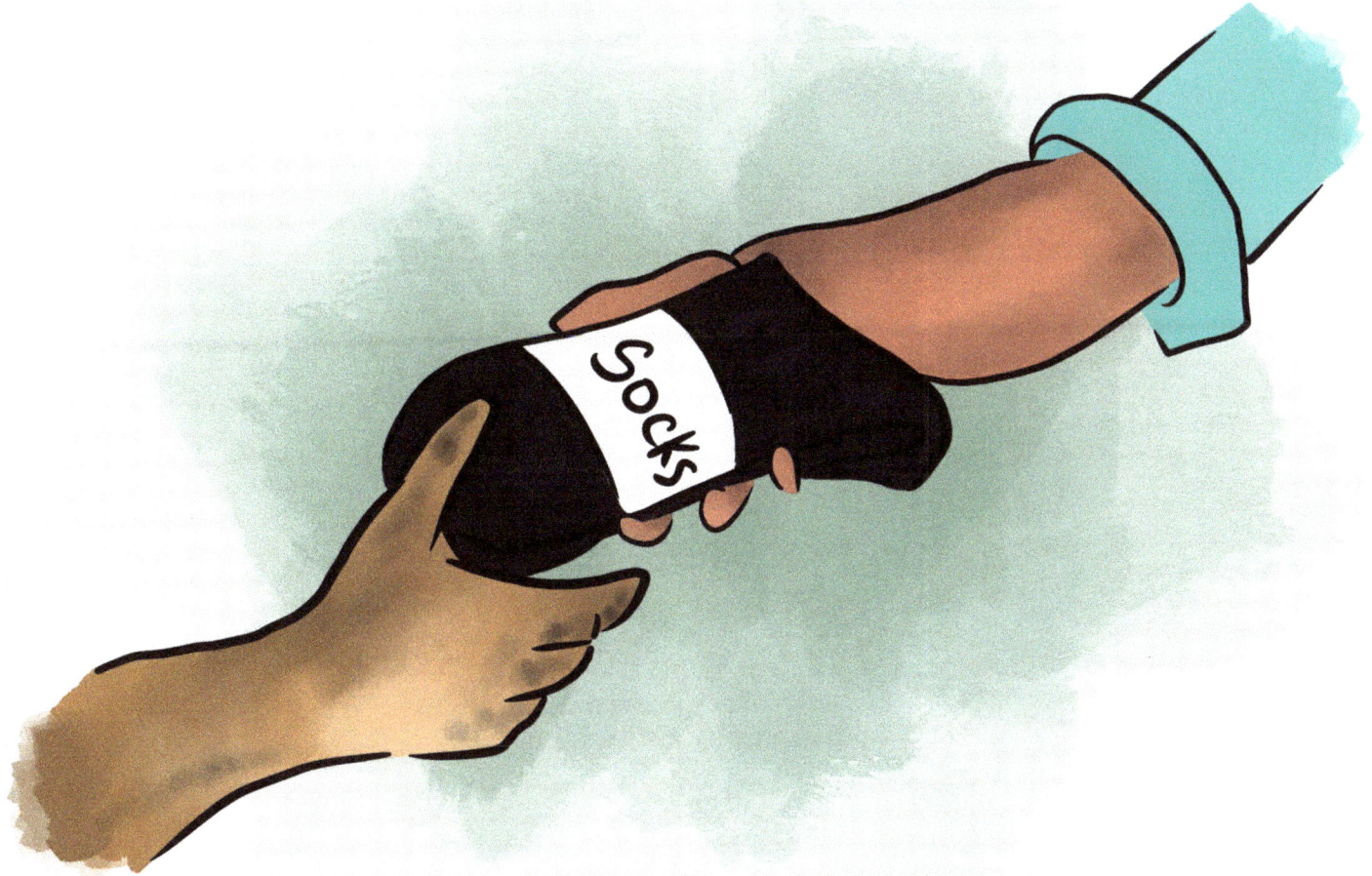

This experience opened Noah's eyes. She did not realize that there were people who lived differently than she did. She immediately went home and started looking around for things she could give away. She and Ms. Worthy went through their clothes to give to others in need.

Noah and her Mom even started volunteering monthly at the local shelter and food pantry. With her Mom by her side, Noah had more conversations, learned more names, and listened to more people. She helped meet the needs that people expressed, not only what she thought they needed.

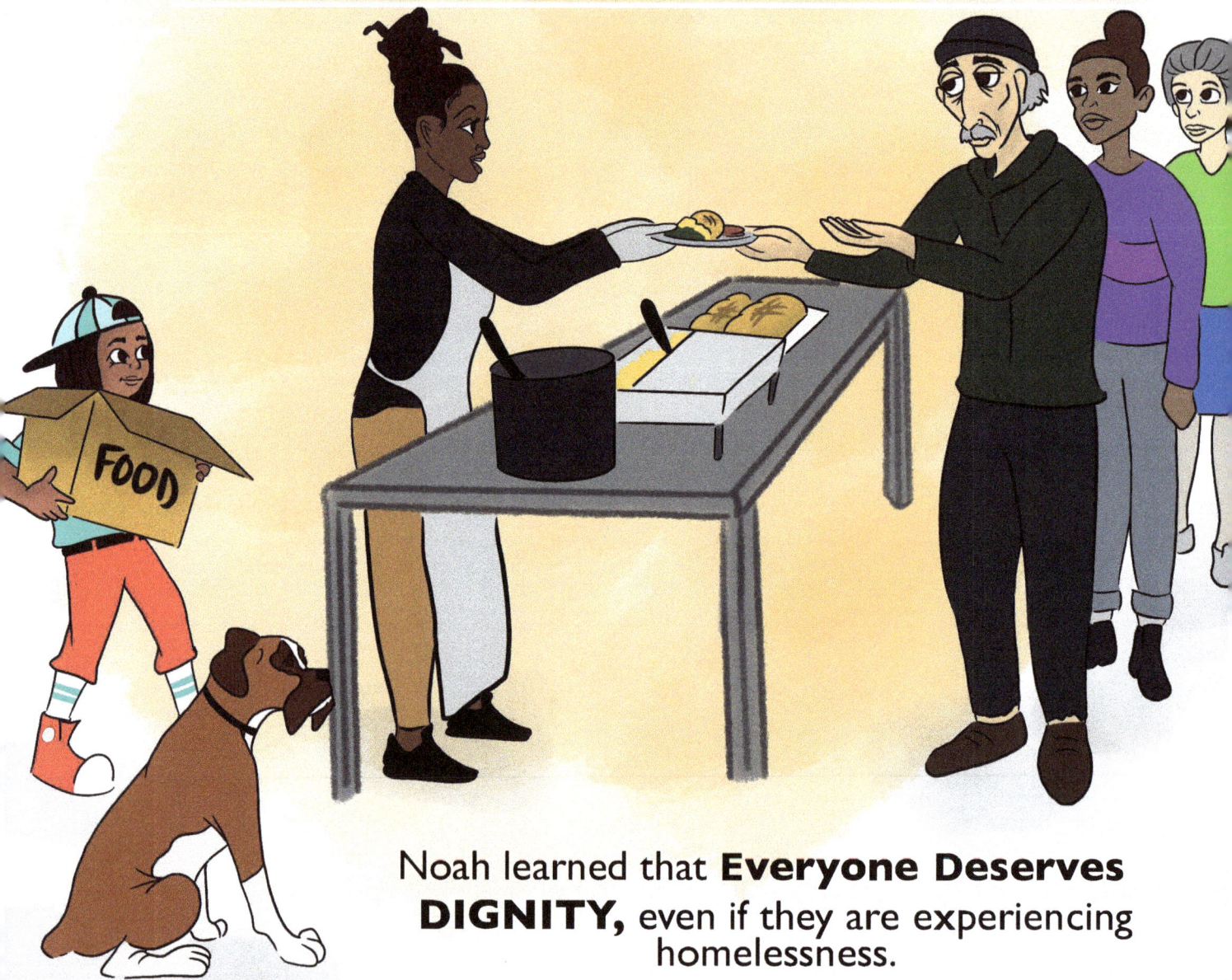

Noah learned that **Everyone Deserves DIGNITY,** even if they are experiencing homelessness.